REMARKS

OF

HON. LYMAN TRUMBULL, OF ILLINOIS,

On seizure of Arsenals at Harper's Ferry, Va., and Liberty, Mo., and in vindication of the Republican Party and its Creed, in response to Senators Chesnut, Yulee, Saulsbury, Clay, and Pugh.

Delivered in the United States Senate, December 6, 7, and 8, 1859.

DECEMBER 6, 1859.

The Senate having under consideration the following resolution, offered by Mr. MASON, of Virginia:

Resolved, That a committee be appointed to inquire into the facts attending the late invasion and seizure of the armory and arsenal of the United States at Harper's Ferry, in Virginia, by a band of armed men, and report whether the same was attended by armed resistance to the authorities and public force of the United States, and by the murder of any of the citizens of Virginia, or of any troops sent there to protect the public property; whether such invasion and seizure was made under color of any organization intended to subvert the Government of any of the States of the Union; what was the character and extent of such organization; and whether any citizens of the United States, not present, were implicated therein or accessory thereto, by contributions of money, arms, munitions, or otherwise; what was the character and extent of the military equipment in the hands or under the control of said armed band, and where and how and when the same was obtained and transported to the place so invaded. And that said committee report whether any and what legislation may, in their opinion, be necessary, on the part of the United States, for the future preservation of the peace of the country, or for the safety of the public property; and that said committee have power to send for persons and papers.

Mr. TRUMBULL said:

Mr. President, when that resolution was offered yesterday, I stated that I would move an amendment to it when it should come up for consideration; but, before proceeding to offer the amendment, I will state that the resolution, as offered by the Senator from Virginia, will receive my support. If any other persons than the twenty-two whose names are known to the country are implicated in, or in any way accessory to, the seizure of Harper's Ferry, and the murder of the citizens of Virginia, let us ascertain who they are, and let them be held responsible for their acts.

I hope this investigation will be thorough and complete. I believe it will do good by disabusing the public mind, in that portion of the Union which feels most sensitively upon this subject, of the idea that the outbreak at Harper's Ferry received any countenance or support from any considerable number of persons in any portion of this Union. No man who is not prepared to subvert the Constitution, destroy the Government, and resolve society into its original elements, can justify such an act. No matter what evils, either real or imaginary, may exist in the body politic, if each individual, or every set of twenty individuals, out of more than twenty millions of people, is to be permitted, in his own way, and in defiance of the laws of the land, to undertake to correct those evils, there is not a Government upon the face of the earth that could last a day. And it seems to me, sir, that those persons who reason only from abstract principles, and believe themselves justifiable on all occasions, and in every form, in combating evil wherever it exists, forget that the right which they claim for themselves exists equally in every other person. All Governments, the best which have been devised, encroach necessarily more or less on the individual rights of man, and to that extent may be regarded as evils. Shall we therefore destroy government, and in place of regulated and constitutional liberty inaugurate a state of anarchy, in which every man shall be permitted to follow the instincts of his own passions or prejudices, and where there will be no protection to the physically weak against the encroachments of the strong? Till we are prepared to inaugurate such a state as this, no man can justify the deeds done at Harper's Ferry.

In regard to the misguided man who led the insurgents on that occasion, I have no remarks to make. He has already expiated upon the gallows the crime which he committed against the laws of his country; and to answer for his errors or his virtues, whatever they may have been, he has gone fearlessly and willingly before that Judge who cannot err; there let us leave him.

The amendment which I propose to offer to the resolution which is pending, and in which, I trust, I may have the support of every Senator, provides for the investigation of a like transaction which occurred in the State of Missouri. I will briefly state what that transaction was, as it may not be fresh in the recollection of Senators.

The Government of the United States had an arsenal at the town of Liberty, in the State of Missouri, of which Captain Leonard had charge. In December, 1855—and the facts which I state appear upon the official records of the country—Captain Leonard testifies that a Judge Thompson, in company with a large number of others, appeared at the arsenal, overpowered him, confined him, broke open the magazines, supplied themselves with cannon, rifles, swords, and pistols, with powder and ball, and took them away from the arsenal. This was followed by the invasion of a peaceful Territory; not twenty-two persons only, but more than a thousand men, marched into the adjoining Territory, armed with weapons taken by violence from an arsenal of the United States, under the charge of an officer of the United States, with the avowed object of making that Territory a slaveholding State. It appears that societies were formed—secret organizations—reaching from Missouri into various States, and, among others, the State of Virginia, whose object and design was by force to introduce Slavery into Kansas; and to carry out this object, these men seized upon these arms and munitions belonging to the Government of the United States. Captain Leonard, in his statement under oath, says:

"The Judge and others told me there were troubles in Kansas, and they wanted arms, but would do nothing wrong with them. I told the Judge this was aggressive on the part of Missouri, and every community was competent to take care of its own affairs, and that the Missourians ought not to interfere. A good deal more was said on both sides, and I felt indignant at the aggression. The Judge himself did not say an uncivil word to me. I had not expected any such thing as this when I first saw the Judge, or I could have had the gates locked.

"The mob proceeded to take arms, forcing the doors, and took three six-pounders, some swords, pistols, rifles, and ammunition, powder, balls, &c., as much as they wanted. They broke some doors open. I do not know how they got the keys to get into the powder magazine, which is composed of brick, and had double doors. Captain Price was the leading man in the crowd, as I understood. Mr. Rout was there. I was kept in the room until the men had got all the arms and ammunition they wanted, and had gone away, Judge Thompson being the last one; when he let me go out, and then he left himself.

"Some six or eight days afterwards, the guns were returned to the arsenal. They were left, I was told, at Col. Allen's place, some three-quarters of a mile from the arsenal. In the mean time, I had reported the facts to Col. Sumner, and he had sent down a company of dragoons. The men sent to me to know if I would receive the arms, and I told them I was not in command, and referred them to Captain Beall, and he told them to bring them along; they did so, and they were received. Among the property taken was some artillery harness; I cannot recollect how many sets. There were some deficiencies in the number of rifles, swords, and pistols, and some harness returned; but I cannot state the precise particulars. These deficiencies have never been made up by the citizens of Missouri; but I have been instructed by Col. Craig, the head of the ordnance department at Washington, to purchase sufficient of such articles as I could obtain in the neighborhood to make up the deficiency, and we did so; but the swords, pistols, and rifles, we have not been able to make up. I do not know how much has been expended in making up this deficiency. Immediately after this robbery, I reported the circumstances to Col. Craig, at Washington, specifying the number and amount of each of the different articles taken. In the course of the winter, he sent me orders to ship the public property to Fort Leavenworth and St. Louis arsenal, giving me a schedule of the amount to be taken to each place, which I did as soon as navigation opened."—*House Report No.* 200, *Thirty-fourth Congress, first session*, pages 1130–31.

It seems that the arsenal at Liberty was broken up, and what remained of the arms were shipped to other military posts. Now, sir, there is a very striking similarity between the breaking into that arsenal and the attack upon the one at Harper's Ferry. The question of Slavery had to do with both. The arsenal in Missouri was broken into for the purpose of obtaining arms to force Slavery upon Kansas; the arsenal at Harper's Ferry was taken possession of for the purpose of expelling Slavery from the State of Virginia—both unjustifiable, and, it seems to me, both proper subjects to be inquired into. Perhaps the latter would never have occurred if inquiry had been made, and the proper steps had been taken when the cry for succor came from Kansas, and her citizens were murdered by the very arms taken from this arsenal or at any rate by persons in the same army with them. Then the complaints that were made were treated as the "shrieks of bleeding Kansas," and they could not be heard. I trust they may get a better hearing now. Now, sir, when the shrieks of Virginia are heard, and the ears of the country are opened, I trust those from Kansas may get a hearing also. I am prepared to hear both; and I hope that the investigation in regard to Harper's Ferry may be impartial, thorough, and complete, and let whoever is implicated in the unlawful transactions there be held responsible; and so, too, in regard to the seizure of the arsenal in the State of Missouri. I offer the following amendment:

After the word "invaded," near the end of the resolution insert:

And that said committee also inquire into the facts attending the invasion, seizure, and robbery, in December, 1855, of the arsenal of the United States, at Liberty, in the State of Missouri, by a mob or body of armed men, and report whether such seizure and robbery was attended by resistance to the authorities of the United States, and followed by an invasion of the Territory of Kansas, and the plunder and murder of any of its inhabitants, or of any citizen of the United States, by the persons who thus seized the arms and ammunition of the Government, or others combined with them, whether said seizure and robbery of the arsenal were made under color of any organization intended to subvert the Government of any of the States or Territories of the Union; what was the character and extent of such organization, and whether any citizens of the United States, not present, were implicated therein, or accessory thereto, by contributions of money, arms, ammunition, or otherwise; what was the character and extent of the military equipments in the hands or under the control of said mob, and how and when and where the same were subsequently used by said mob; what was the value of the arms and ammunition of every description so taken from the said arsenal by the mob; whether the same or any part thereof have been returned, and the value of such as were lost; whether Captain Luther Leonard, the United States officer in command of the arsenal, communicated the facts in relation to its seizure and robbery to his superior officer, and what measures, if any, were taken in reference thereto.

DECEMBER 7, 1859.

Mr. PUGH, of Ohio, having made an appeal to Mr. TRUMBULL to withdraw his amendment,

Mr. TRUMBULL said:

After what has been said, particularly by the Senator who last addressed the Senate, [Mr. CHESNUT,] in regard to the apprehension that something may be drawn out in the course of this investigation which may fasten the insurrection at Harper's Ferry upon the Republican party, and it appearing, also, by the statements of the Senators from Virginia, that the object of this resolution is to ascertain the public sentiment of the North, I am a little astonished that any person can ask me to withdraw an amendment which will lead also to ascertaining what the sentiment of the South may be.

I have been appealed to to state why this amendment was offered. I will tell you, sir, and it will be but a repetition of what I stated yesterday. I believe the outbreak at Harper's Ferry has arisen, not from the teachings and the acts of the Republican party, or any of its leaders, or anybody in its ranks, as the Senator from South Carolina supposes, but from the teachings of the party with which he himself is associated. The

Democratic party, by upholding and never rebuking the sacking of the arsenal in Missouri, by rewarding with office the men who did it, by sending the Federal troops, they having control of the Government at the time, into Kansas, to hold in confinement men indicted upon trumped-up charges of treason, set an example to the country which engendered the spirit that maddened Brown. I need not and will not go over the history of that transaction, which the Senator from Wisconsin has just detailed. I offered the amendment in good faith, as being pertinent to the original resolution, as properly connected with it, as relating to a similar transaction.

But it is asked why I did not call for this investigation five years ago. Well, to begin with, the occurrence was only four years since. But of what use would it have been for me to have moved in the Senate for a committee of investigation? Does the Senator from South Carolina suppose that the Senate or the country has forgotten how everything relating to Kansas was managed here? A proposition offered in the Senate of the United States to inquire into these matters would have been scouted at the time. I recollect that I offered several propositions in order to remedy the difficulties in Kansas, not one of which received the sanction of the Senate. I proposed to repeal the laws abridging the freedom of speech in Kansas—laws which subjected a man to imprisonment for years who should venture to say that Slavery did not exist in that Territory. All my propositions were voted down.

There was a condition of things then existing that would have made any effort in this body to raise a committee of this kind perfectly useless. Now, however, a different feeling prevails. Another arsenal has been taken possession of. There is a difference between the two cases. I do not understand that the arms of the Government at Harper's Ferry were appropriated to the use of the insurgents, but in Missouri the public arms were carried away, part have never been returned, and the officer in command was directed to supply other portions by purchase, which he has done.

I think that the two things properly go together, and that one should be inquired into as much as the other. As great an outrage was committed four years ago, in taking possession of the arsenal at Liberty, as was committed a month or two ago, in taking possession of the armory at Harper's Ferry. I apprehend that where hundreds of dollars worth of property were destroyed at Harper's Ferry, thousands were destroyed in consequence of the taking possession of the arsenal at Liberty. I apprehend that where one life was lost in consequence of the acts at Harper's Ferry, many lives were lost in consequence of the taking possession of the arsenal at Liberty and the events that followed it. Sir, it was with the arms which were supplied from that arsenal that Lawrence was besieged. The army that encamped at Wakarusa were armed with weapons from the United States arsenal, to what extent I am unable to say. I should like to see the official report that was made to the War Department at the time this transaction occurred. I recollect that we passed resolutions calling upon the President, or upon the proper Department, and probably upon both, for all the papers and correspondence in regard to these matters, but I have no recollection of having ever seen the official report of the officer commanding at Liberty at the time the arsenal was taken possession of by this Missouri mob.

Now, sir, as I am up, I will reply to some of the statements of the Senator from South Carolina. He says that he claims only that which is the right of the South—the right to take slaves to the common Territories of the United States. Sir, they have no such right. We do not deny the equality of the States which hold slaves. I am as much for maintaining the equality of the States of the Union as the Senator from South Carolina; but what on earth has the introduction of Slavery into a Territory to do with the rights of any State, North or South? Has any State, as a State, a right to take a slave into a Territory? The Senator will not pretend that. Then why talk about State rights? The most that can be claimed is, that individuals residing in different States of the Union may take their property, if it happens to be in slaves, into the Territories. Well, that is not a State right; it is an individual right, if it exists at all. We do not propose to impose on the Senator from South Carolina, or any of his constituents, an inequality in that respect. If he cannot take a slave into the Territory of Kansas, neither can I. If the citizens of South Carolina cannot take Slavery there, neither can the citizens of Illinois. The rights of each State are precisely the same.

Now, you of the South are threatening to dissolve the Union, and break up the Confederacy, because, as you charge, the Northern people are assailants and aggressors on your rights. Is the whole history of this country forgotten? How is it, that the moment this Government was formed, one of the first acts of the men who made it was to provide that Slavery should not go into the Territories belonging to the United States? Is it possible that the men who made this Government would, in the first Congress that met under it, pass a law so unjust to a portion of the States of the Union as to justify their breaking it up? How was it that South Carolina herself agreed to exclude Slavery from the State, then Territory, which I have the honor, in part, to represent?

Sir, we lived under this policy; the great Northwest was settled under this policy of excluding Slavery from the Territories of the United States; and how is it that neither South Carolina nor Virginia found out that they were not treated as equals in this Confederacy? Why, sir, at so late a period as 1848, when a Southern man was President of the United States, Congress, by direct act, excluded Slavery from Oregon. Now, can it be that there is any such thing as inequality or injustice to any State of this Union in the exclusion of Slavery from a Territory? Will the Senator from South Carolina do his ancestors the injustice to believe that they submitted to the degradation and dishonor, as he now calls it, of being excluded from the common Territories of the country? Sir, they chose it, not as a degradation, not as a dishonor, but for wise purposes, and to accomplish great ends. The founders of our Government were men who, in their day, believed the institution of Slavery to be an evil in the country. They found it here. They did not see the means of getting rid of it immediately. They would not abolish it at once. They conferred upon the Federal Government no power to interfere with it in the States which formed the Federal Government; but they gave power to this Federal Government to prevent its extension. They took steps immediately after the Government was organized to prevent Slavery from going into any portion of the territory then belonging to the United States. I know, sir, that Slavery went into Tennessee, Mississippi, and other States, but it went there in defiance of the Federal Government. The territories composing those States were ceded to the United States on condition that the United States should not exclude Slavery from them; but the territory northwest of the river Ohio was ceded without any such condition, and Congress immediately excluded Slavery, with the acquiescence of the South—yea, sir, the South itself moving in the matter; and your own great man, the great statesman of America, himself is the author of the provision which excluded Slavery from the Northwestern Territory.

We deny that there is any disposition in any portion of the North to treat the South as unequals in this common Confederacy.

Having shown that to some extent, I wish to come back, and inquire of the Senator from South Carolina, and his associates, what is the meaning of the resolutions adopted in the Southern States, and of the speeches made by prominent men in the Southern States, in which they declare that in case a certain individual is elected President of these United States, in a constitutional way, or in case the Republican party elect a President of the United States, that they will take steps for the formation of a Southern Confederacy and the dissolution of the Union. Is not that treating us as unequals? What do you mean by it? You come into the Senate of the United States, and charge the North with acting unequally and unjustly towards you; and yet you say to the North, "although we have united together in a common Confederacy, in which we have agreed that the Chief Magistrate shall be elected in a particular way, and by a majority expressed in the constitutional form, yet, if you so elect a man, we will break up the Government!" What is that but saying, "we are your superiors, and your majority shall submit to what the minority think proper to dictate?"

Mr. CHESNUT. Does the Senator desire an answer now?

Mr. TRUMBULL. Yes, sir.

Mr. CHESNUT. I will simply state, so far as it is within my knowledge, what I believe to be the meaning of that declaration. It is not charging the North with inferiority. The declarations having been made by those who entertain them, I presume go upon the ground of a distinct, unmistakable, clear enunciation of principles—principles which subvert the Constitution of the United States, the rights and equality of the States, and which are held up in advance to us, that "this will be our programme; this will be the course of action that we will pursue, and we notify you in advance." Now, sir, what is that programme? What have they announced to us as the "irrepressible conflict?" Does the Senator suppose that when the distinguished leader of that party announced to the world that the wheat-fields and the rye-fields of Massachusetts and New York must ultimately be tilled by slave labor, that he meant any such thing—that he supposed for a moment that that was to be the result of this "irrepressible conflict?" No, sir; but the other branch of the alternative—that the sugar plantations of Louisiana and the cotton and rice plantations of South Carolina shall be tilled by free labor, and by free labor only. That is a declaration of war.

It is a declaration against the rights of the people, secured by the compact and the Constitution of the country, and we are forewarned. Notwithstanding this may be a constitutional election, that a majority, according to the prescribed forms of the Constitution, have a right to elect, and the election is valid, yet, rather than submit to a fate forewarned, they who think so give timely notice that they do not intend to submit to it. It is a degradation by a proclamation in advance, to be met by a counter-proclamation, without touching the inferiority of the Northern States at all. Sir, it is not the men, it is not the party, it is not the States, but it is the principle, that "we subjugate you; give us the reins of power, and we will place you at our feet; we will take from you what you have, quietly if you will yield, forcibly if you do not; and we will hold you under the power of this Federal Government, subject to the domination of a party whose principles are in violation," according to our judgment, "of every principle of the Constitution." That, I presume, is the meaning of those who profess that sentiment.

Mr. TRUMBULL. Mr. President, it is just such speeches as this we have listened to from the Senator from South Carolina, based upon a misunderstanding of the Republican party of the North, that has misled the South. The North intends no encroachment upon the South. The Republican party is a party, in its principles, public and avowed to the world, and it is because of the misrepresentation of the objects and views of that party that the prejudices of the South have been excited against it, and chiefly by the misrepresentations which have been made by this so-called Democratic party in the North. They choose to call every person that does not unite with them an Abolitionist.

I was born and bred up in the Democratic faith, acted with the Democratic party, sustained its measures and its men upon principle when that party was divided from the Whig party upon questions of finance, in regard to the commercial interests of the country, and other great questions. But, in 1854, what was done? I was one of those who acquiesced in the measures of 1850, and agreed to abide by the settlement then made. I heard with delight the declaration of Franklin Pierce, when inaugurated President, and in his message, that the settlement of 1850 should suffer no shock which he could prevent during his Administration. I was glad when the Kansas-Nebraska bill was introduced, accompanied by the report of a committee in this body, declaring that to repeal the Missouri compromise would be a departure from the measures of 1850. It was said that the compromise measures of 1850 had given peace to the country; that the Slavery question was forever afterwards to be banished from the Halls of Congress, and that no man was to be tolerated who should under any pretence whatever, in Congress or out of Congress, attempt to stir up again this exciting question.

I, in good faith, supposed that these declarations meant something; and therefore when, in 1854, notwithstanding these assurances to the country, the proposition was sprung upon it to repeal the Missouri compromise, and open Kansas to Slavery, and when the measure was made the test and the only test of party faith, I did refuse to co-operate with the party which made that the only test of its political faith. Then it was that the old Democratic party and the Whig party were broken up. They were both disbanded, and a new question was thrust upon the country, which had not before been in issue between parties. When it was thrust upon us, and parties and persons took issue upon the question of the repeal of the Missouri compromise and the opening of Kansas to Slavery, I united with that party which took ground against the repeal of the Missouri compromise, and in favor of standing by what all parties had agreed to but four years previous—ay, sir, but two years previous, when they nominated their respective candidates for the Presidency. To style the party that now calls itself Democratic, the successor of the old Democratic party, is a misnomer. It is no more the successor of that party than the Republican party. The country seems to have forgotten, and gentlemen who use this word "Democratic," as if it had some meaning, at this day, seem to have forgotten that a majority of the members of the House of Representatives from the Northern States of the Democratic party voted against the repeal of the Missouri compromise. It was a minority of the Democratic party that favored that measure, and then it was that these new parties were formed, composed of persons who had before belonged indiscriminately either to the Whig or the Democratic party.

When the Senator from South Carolina attributes to the Republican party of the North the views which he does, he entirely misapprehends the views of that party. They have been reiterated a hundred times. I wish I had a voice that I could reiterate them so that every man in the South should hear. I would say to every man from the Gulf to the Potomac, the Republican party plants itself on this Slavery question precisely on the ground upon which your own Washington and Jefferson stood. We avow in our platform of principles that we will abide by the Constitution. We have no intention of interfering with your domestic institutions; and when the Senator from South Carolina talks about the North interfering with the institutions of the South, I ask when, where? Never, sir. "Oh! but you exclude us from the common territory." Is that an interference with your institutions? Was it an interference in 1787? Was it an interference in 1789, when your own great men passed the act to exclude Slavery from the Territories? You did not so regard it. Did those men put a dishonor upon themselves? We believe that these Territories are the common property of the United States, as much as you; we tell you that a man who has no slaves has as much right to go there as a man who has slaves; that one has just as much right to settle in the Territories of the United States as another; but we tell you that no man can take the institutions of his State, along with him wherever he goes. When he goes beyond the jurisdiction of his State, and enters some other jurisdiction, the local laws which governed him in the State whence he emigrated cease to operate.

The Constitution of the United States has expressly conferred upon Congress authority to govern these Territories, and the authority has always been exercised. It is altogether a mistaken notion that any inequality is put upon Southern men by refusing to extend Slavery into the Territories. Why, sir, in the Southern States, a majority of your white population are not slaveholders. Not one in ten, only about one in twenty of your population own slaves, and if you will divide them into families, I suppose that not one family in five in all the Southern States owns a slave. We believe that it is for the interests of this great country, for the interests of the people who are to settle our Territories, that they should be settled by free white people. What interest have four families out of five in the Southern States in introducing Slavery into Kansas, or into any free territory? Will you tell me that it is putting a degradation on them, unless they are permitted to introduce slaves into the Territories? They have none to introduce. They do not want Slavery. Nine out of ten of your white population in Carolina own no slaves, and at least four out of five of the families of that State, I presume, have no slaves. Is it a degradation then upon them? Who is it upon? Why, if on any one, it is on your one-twentieth person; and legislation to protect his interests, at the expense of nineteen-twentieths, is to be brought about in the name of Democracy. I said a degradation upon the one-twentieth person. It is no degradation upon him. It is no degradation upon any man. You of the South, as citizens of this common country, are as much interested in keeping the Territories free as we of the North. Most of your people own no slaves, and, as a matter of course, would prefer, when they emigrate, to come into a non-slaveholding country. The State in which I reside has in it hundreds and thousands and tens of thousands of people from the slaveholding States. They want no Slavery, and I suppose if the question were to be submitted to the citizens of Illinois to-morrow, whether Slavery should be introduced, although there are thousands of voters from Maryland, Virginia, Kentucky, Tennessee, North Carolina, Georgia, and South Carolina, it would not get one vote in ten thousand in the State.

Mr. YULEE. Will the Senator allow me to interrupt him a moment?

Mr. TRUMBULL. Yes, sir.

Mr. YULEE. The Senator undertook just

now to enlighten us in respect to the attitude of the party of which he is a member upon this slave question. I am very solicitous to know precisely where the Senator's party stands upon that question, and what is the purpose of the organization, for I understand the organization to refer mainly to the question of Slavery. I desire to know the precise position of the party to which the Senator belongs, and which principally prevails in the Northern States on that subject.

Mr. TRUMBULL. If the Senator from Florida cannot understand the principles of the Republican party, which have been proclaimed and published to the world, he is certainly not a very apt scholar, and I shall almost despair of enlightening him. Our principles are emblazoned before the country and published in the platforms of the party. Did he never read them, or has he gone on, without reading our principles, and misunderstanding them?

Mr. YULEE. I have certainly read them; but, unfortunately, never understood them.

Mr. TRUMBULL. Then, if I can be the means of enlightening my friend from Florida as to any particular part of our platform that he cannot understand, it will afford me great pleasure to do so.

Mr. WADE. I think it will take until morning to do this, and I therefore move that the Senate do now adjourn.

The motion was agreed to; and the Senate adjourned.

DECEMBER 8, 1859.

Mr. TRUMBULL said:

Mr. President, just before the adjournment of this body yesterday, I was called upon by the Senator from Florida [Mr. YULEE] to state what were the principles of the Republican party.

Sir, I did suppose that the Senator from Florida, and every Senator, could understand, if he desired to do so, what our principles were. They have been proclaimed by an authoritative Convention of the party, in language as plain as it is in the power of man to employ; and it is only by mystification, by misrepresentations of them in many portions of the country, as I think, that the public mind of the South has been excited against the Republican party. I have brought along with me their declaration of principles, and, so far as it relates to the Slavery question, I will read it; it is brief, and I should like to know to what portion of it the Senator from Florida, or any other Senator or individual, North or South, objects. Here it is:

"*Resolved*, That the maintenance of the principles promulgated in the Declaration of Independence, and embodied in the Federal Constitution, are essential to the preservation of our Republican institutions, and that the Federal Constitution, the rights of the States, and the Union of the States, must and shall be preserved."

Does the Senator from Florida understand that—that the Constitution of the United States, the rights of the States, and the principles embodied in the Constitution, must and shall be preserved?

Mr. YULEE. I want to know how you construe the Constitution?

Mr. TRUMBULL. We will tell you. We say ourselves how we construe it on the Slavery question:

"*Resolved*, That, with our republican fathers, we hold it to be a self-evident truth that all men are endowed with the inalienable right of life, liberty, and the pursuit of happiness; and that the primary object and ulterior design of our Federal Government is, to grant these rights to all persons under its exclusive jurisdiction. That as our republican fathers, when they had abolished Slavery in all our national territory, ordained that no person shall be deprived of life, liberty, or property, without due process of law, it becomes our duty to maintain this provision of the Constitution (against all attempts to violate it for the purpose of establishing Slavery in the Territories of the United States) by positive legislation prohibiting its existence or extension therein. That we deny the authority of Congress, of a Territorial Legislature, of any individual or association of individuals, to give legal existence to Slavery in any Territory of the United States, while the present Constitution shall be maintained.

"*Resolved*, That the Constitution confers upon Congress sovereign power over the Territories of the United States, for their government; and that, in the exercise of this power, it is both the right and the imperative duty of Congress to prohibit in the Territories those twin relics of barbarism, Polygamy and Slavery."

That is the whole platform of the Republican party on the subject of Slavery.

Mr. SAULSBURY. Will the Senator from Illinois allow me to ask him a question?

Mr. TRUMBULL. Yes, sir.

Mr. SAULSBURY. If it be true, as that last resolution states, that the Constitution confers upon Congress sovereign power over the Territories of the United States, for their government, why is it that that power, which the resolution declares to be sovereign in Congress—by which, I presume, is meant a supreme power, a power which has no superior—is not capable of being exercised for the establishment of Slavery in a Territory, as well as for the prohibition of Slavery in a Territory?

Mr. TRUMBULL. Mr. President, the power which the Federal Government may exercise over a Territory is sovereign power in its government, as we all know and understand, within the Constitution of the United States. The Constitution of the United States declares that Congress shall pass no law establishing any particular form of religion or abridging the freedom of speech or of the press. I readily admit, and so does the Republican party, that the Congress of the United States cannot pass a law abridging the freedom of speech in any one of the Territories. They are expressly prohibited from so doing. They have the sovereign power over the Territories, to legislate for them in all matters within the Constitution of the United States; and the Constitution of the United States does not authorize Congress to establish Slavery. The Constitution is based upon this principle. It does not establish Slavery at all, but merely tolerates it where it already exists by virtue of State laws. That is the meaning of the Constitution of the United States. It is a Constitution of Freedom, the word "slave" not occurring in it, and the men who framed the Constitution believed that in the process of time there would be no slaves in any portion of the Confederacy, and one of its principal authors objected to the use of the word "slave," lest future generations might know that there was Slavery in some of the States when the Constitution was formed. If you will turn to that clause of the Constitution relating to the reclamation of fugitive slaves, you will find that it reads, that "no person held to service or labor in one State, under the laws thereof," that is, under the laws of the State, "escaping into another, shall, in consequence of any law or regulation therein, be discharged from such service or labor, but shall be delivered up." There is no provision for the delivering up of a man who is held to service by any other than a State law. If held to service by virtue of the Constitution, that instrument contains no provision for his return when he escapes from one State to another. This shows that the framers of the Constitution never contemplated that a person could be held to service, whether as a slave or as an apprentice, except by virtue of State laws, else the provision for reclamation would have been general, and not limited to persons so held. Would the Senator from Delaware contend that, under this clause of the Constitution, he could reclaim a person held as a slave, by virtue of that instrument, who had escaped from one State into another? Suppose a person comes into the State of Delaware, who, it is contended, is a slave, and his alleged owner comes to reclaim him—would you give him up if he did not show that he was held as a slave under the laws of the State from which he escaped? If you would not, then, as a matter of course, you could not give up a person who was held as a slave in one of the Territories, because he could not be so held in a Territory by virtue of any State law.

Lest I be misunderstood, I will state that I do not mean to say that if there is Slavery in one of the Territories of the Union, as there was by the acquiescence of Congress in Tennessee and Kentucky and in the Southwestern States while they were Territories, a negro who is held as a slave there, and escapes into any of the States of the Union, may not be reclaimed. I hold to no such doctrine. I contend that the Congress of the United States have sovereign power over the Territories, to legislate for them within the Constitution, and had the right to provide, as it did in the enactment of the ordinance of 1787 for the Northwestern Territory, that fugitives who should escape to that Territory from slaveholding States should be surrendered up. It is by virtue of its sovereign power over the Territories, and not by virtue of the clause of the Constitution relating to the return of fugitives from one *State* to another, that Congress provides a law by which a person held to service or labor in a slaveholding Territory may be reclaimed when he escapes into a State, and by which a slave in a State who escapes into a free Territory may be reclaimed and brought back to the State whence he fled.

Now, sir, what portion of this platform or creed does the Senator from Florida object to? I know what he will say. He objects to that part which excludes Slavery from the Territories. Is there any other?

Mr. YULEE. I desire to hear from the Senator an illustration and exposition of his creed; whether he intends us to understand, or his party intend it to be understood, that by the Constitution of the United States property in slaves was abolished, and stands abolished in all national territory, and in all territory over which we have exclusive jurisdiction. Does he mean to say that the tenure in slave property in the District of Columbia, and in the forts and in the arsenals, as well as in the Territories of the United States, was abolished under the Constitution, and stands abolished now?

If there be any meaning in this platform, it is a meaning which strikes at the root of property in slaves in all the new States of this Confederacy. The ground upon which you rest yourself is, that it is not only not in the power of Congress, but that it is not in the power of a Territorial Government or of any association of individuals, under any pretext or in any form, to give existence to Slavery in a Territory. If that be so, all the slaves in Louisiana, all the slaves in Tennessee, in Missouri, in every other new State of this Confederacy, were free by virtue of the Constitution, and are illegally held.

When the Senator attempts to present to us here a principle by which his party is to be ruled, we have a right to ask him, and to know, by what practical measures of legislation his party propose to give effect to the principle which they undertake to assert. Now, let us take the case of a Territory immediately occupied by emigrants from a Southern State, and by them alone, accompanied with their slave property, which the Supreme Court declares to be legally their property there—I wish to know by what practical measure of legislation the Senator proposes to give effect to his principle. Is it by a code to abolish the property of the slaveholder in his slaves there? Is that what he proposes to do? If the people of the Territory desire to use that form of labor, does he mean to deny them that right, and to deny it by an act of the Federal Legislature prohibiting the enjoyment of that right to the inhabitants of the Territory?

More than that; if, when they come to form themselves into a sovereign community, and present themselves here, under the Federal Constitution, for admission as a State of this Union, with a clause in their Constitution protecting slave property, I wish to know whether it is a part of the policy and purpose of the party of which the Senator is a member, giving effect to the principle here asserted as their rule of action, to reject the application.

If the end and aim of the Senator's organization is limited to the Territorial question, and when that is done with, all is done with it on the slave question, then the South will know, so far, what to expect from them.

Next, so far as the Territorial question is concerned, I ask the Senator to give us the practical measures by which they propose to give application to their principles, and to tell us upon what ground they assert that property in slaves is abolished by the Constitution, and yet justify a continued recognition of that right in the District of Columbia, the forts and arsenals, and those of the Territories of the United States in which it has been permitted, not only by the acquiescence but by the direct authority of law, to exist, for such was the case in Tennessee, and in other portions of the new States. Congress did, by express enactment, authorize the existence of Slavery. I yield to the Senator.

Mr. TRUMBULL. Mr. President, I am glad this discussion has arisen. I have no right to impeach the motives of gentlemen on the other side; I suppose they really labor under some misapprehension in regard to our principles. I think, if we could understand each other, the good old times, when a man from the South and a man from the North could meet together in a friendly spirit, without any dispute upon this question, would return. I think misapprehension is the foundation of the great controversy upon the Slavery question.

The Senator has thought proper to speak of the South. He speaks of the degradation, as he calls it, to the South, of excluding them from a Territory——

Mr. YULEE. That was the Senator's own word. I merely quoted his own language.

Mr. TRUMBULL. We mean no degradation to the South. I am sorry that the word "South" has been used with regard to this alleged right to extend Slavery to a Territory. I tried yesterday to explain that the South is made up of a great many persons who are not slaveholders, by far many more than the slaveholders, and therefore I do not know what right those who hold slaves have to arrogate to themselves that they are the South. They are a portion of the South, and a small portion only, about one-twentieth part, as shown by the census.

The Senator asks if this platform of principles is only intended to apply to the Territories. Most assuredly the Republican party had its origin in the question of Slavery in regard to the Territories. It was the departure from the policy of this Government, from the day of its foundation down to 1854, which gave rise to the Republican party. It was an organization in reference to the question of Slavery in the Territories, and nowhere else. There is nothing in this platform in regard to the question of Slavery in the States of this Union; and, lest I forget it, permit me to say that I speak not for the Republican party, except as its platform speaks. I claim no authority to be its exponent. Its exponent is its principles, as declared here in this document.

Mr. YULEE. I desire to have his exposition of the platform, or what he presents as his platform.

Mr. TRUMBULL. The Senator speaks of what I *present* as the platform. Now, is it possible that the Senator from Florida has not seen, and does not know, this platform? Is there any other? Why say, "what I present as the platform?" Why not say, "the platform of the Republican party?" Why should we seek here, in the Senate of the United States, to mislead anybody? I am sorry we cannot speak of admitted facts, as they are. We are trying here, I trust, to arrive at an understanding with each other. That is my object; and I wish to do away with all these clap-trap expressions and these ugly names that are used for the purpose of exciting prejudice. Why is it that members of the Senate of the United States, and that the Cabinet officers of the country, talk of the Republican party as the Black Republican party? Do they want to create a prejudice against it? The Senator did not use that word.

Mr. YULEE. No, I did not use it.

Mr. TRUMBULL. I happened to speak of it now—it has been used in this debate—because the Senator seemed to cast a suspicion upon the platform. Why, sir, there is but the one.

Mr. YULEE. It may be. I would state here to the Senator, that I did not use the term Black Republican.

Mr. TRUMBULL. I have said you did not.

Mr. YULEE. But I did not use the term Republican here, for the reason, as I said last night, that that term and that party denomination having been once consecrated by a national party of far other, and, as I humbly think, higher objects than the present party, no party, whatever its objects may be, has the right to appropriate that name. It has become the property of a preceding party, and therefore some qualification of the term Republican, by which the gentleman's party may be defined, ought to be adopted. I will not myself apply a qualification, but leave it to that party to discover, as I hope they will, some qualification of the term Republican.

Mr. TRUMBULL. Mr. President, it is because we advocate every principle advocated by the old Republican party that we adopt its name; and I say to the Senator to-day, show me a departure from the principles of the Republican party of Thomas Jefferson's days, and I will oppose that departure in the Republican party of to-day. It is because we advocate the principles of Thomas Jefferson, because we advocate the principles of the Republican party of 1800, that we call ourselves Republicans; and, if I know myself, I will adhere to the principles of the old Republican party in regard to this question. The father of that party is our great model. Our principles are taken from him. The very words of our platform which the gentleman objects to, were indited by his hand.

Mr. YULEE. "To create, not to destroy, a free government?"

Mr. TRUMBULL. Yes, sir; and we will perpetuate free government by continuing the principles that he advocated. But, sir, what beyond that? How has it come, from a gentleman upon that side of the House, to tell us we must not call ourselves Republicans, when they assume to call themselves Democrats? Democrats! And the illustration of your principle, democracy, is the supremacy of an aristocracy of slaveholders in this country. Any man can be a member of the Democratic party who will adopt your creed on the subject of the spread of Slavery, and the upholding of slaveholding institutions in this country, which concern directly not one man in sixty of the population of this Union. That is the party that has arrogated to itself the name of "Democrat," and that reproaches us for calling ourselves Republicans. Democrats! A party that legislates for the interest of one out of sixty—forgetting the interest of four-fifths of the families of the South to promote that of one-fifth.

The Senator wishes to know if Slavery was abolished by the Constitution of the United States. I have already said, no; Slavery was not abolished by the Constitution of the United States. I stated before, and I will try to repeat it again, that the Constitution was based upon the idea of Freedom, but it did not abolish Slavery where it existed by State or local law. It did not interfere to do that. It allowed the

States to manage that for themselves, and provided that, when one held to service should escape to another State, where Slavery did not exist, he might be reclaimed; and I wish the Senator to understand from me that I acquiesce in that clause of the Constitution of the United States. I recognise your right to reclaim the person who runs away, but I think it should be done in a judicious and proper manner, without exciting bad feeling in the country.

Mr. CLAY. Will the Senator allow me a moment, to ask him whether he recognises the right to reclaim fugitive slaves in the Territories?

Mr. TRUMBULL. I do, under an act of Congress applicable to Territories.

Mr. CLAY. Then I will ask him to reconcile the apparent discrepancy between the platform from which he has read and the position he now assumes; for in that platform, as he read it, it is declared that neither Congress nor any individual can give any legal assistance to Slavery within the Territories.

Mr. TRUMBULL. "Give legal existence to Slavery in a Territory," is the language. We deny that the right to reclaim a fugitive proves the existence of Slavery in a Territory, any more than it does in a State. We have expressly provided by our Constitution, in the State of Illinois, that Slavery shall not exist there, and yet I will say to the Senator from Alabama, that if a slave of his escapes to the State of Illinois, we recognise the right of the owner to reclaim him, and I recognise the same right in a Territory.

Mr. CLAY. If the Senator will pardon me for interrupting him, I will say that in the platform of that party from which I just now read, the word is "assistance," not "existence;" and I have never yet, in any platform of that party which has come under my view, seen the word "existence." It is "assistance." It is so published in that which I have before me, and I have never seen it otherwise.

Mr. TRUMBULL. The word is "existence" in the platform as I have it, and I never understood it to be otherwise. I have the platform as used in the Northern States. If it has been differently published, I was not aware of it.

Mr. CLAY. Still, if the Senator will pardon me, suppose the copy I have is wrong, and the word should be "existence," as claimed by him, I ask him, then, how he can reconcile with his theory, as proclaimed in this platform, of the right of all men to liberty, and the obligation of the Federal Government to secure that right within the Territories, the countervailing obligation to restore a fugitive slave.

Mr. TRUMBULL. Mr. President, I will try to do so. I will give him my understanding of it as calmly and impartially as I am able. I understand that part of the platform to be the assertion of a great natural right, and that is what I understand by those words in the Declaration of Independence, wherein it is declared that "all men are created equal, and endowed by their Creator," not by the Government, "with certain inalienable rights, among which are life, liberty and the pursuit of happiness." Now, I do not understand that our fathers supposed they could carry out these principles perfectly in government. Every Government, as I had occasion to say in this debate before, is an encroachment, more or less, on the natural rights of man. What did they mean? Why, sir, the men who signed their names to that immortal Declaration of Independence were men who either themselves or their ancestors had fled from despotisms in the Old World. They had seen men claiming to rule by Divine right as kings; they had seen another class of men claiming to rule and lord it over the mass of their fellow-beings by hereditary right, and they intended to put it upon record in this formation of the Government which they were making, that their posterity in all time might know that they recognised no Divine right of one man over another, no hereditary right of lords and nobles to trample upon their fellow men. Naturally, no such right can exist. It is but the assertion of power growing out of the organization of Governments. Our ancestors intended to form a Government as near the great principles of natural right as they could. As Mr. Jefferson said, the most perfect Government on earth would be one which secured to honest labor the fruits of its own industry, and interfered no more than was necessary to prevent anarchy, or the encroachments of the strong upon the weak. I do not quote his beautiful language, but the idea. This is what I understand to be meant by this platform of principles in that respect.

Mr. CLAY. Will the Senator pardon me for asking him a further question?

Mr. TRUMBULL. Undoubtedly.

Mr. CLAY. I do not mean to interrupt him; but as he seems disposed to be candid and communicative, I will trouble him with a further question. I would be glad if he can explain how he can reconcile with the personal integrity of the framers of the Declaration of Independence and the Federal Constitution, their holding slaves, and retaining them as slaves, and distributing them by their last will and testament among their children, with their declaration that those men were entitled to life and liberty; and if he can reconcile these matters, I would ask him, furthermore, whether he understands the words of the Declaration of Independence, or of the Federal Constitution, which declares that the Constitution was formed for ourselves and our posterity, to embrace also the negroes.

Mr. TRUMBULL. I reconcile what seems to the gentleman to be a contradiction in this way: Our fathers had to deal with circumstances as they were. They declared great fundamental principles. The Senator from Alabama will agree with me, that any evil is wrong; that any encroachment upon the natural rights of any of us (and our Government restrains us more or less) is only to be justified upon the ground that it is necessary for organized society and for government, and that men could not live together, except in eternal quarrels, unless we had a government of some kind; but that does not militate against the truth that the great Author of all created us equal and with the same rights.

Mr. CLAY. The Senator does not seem to apprehend the force of my question. Perhaps I did not put it fairly. According to the declaration in your platform, as read, I understand your party to maintain that the negro enjoys, in common with the white man, an inalienable right to liberty. You denounce the violation of that right as a crime, a sin in the eye of Heaven, and a crime against the laws of man; a violation of the doctrines of Christianity. You denounce it as a twin relic of barbarism with polygamy. Now, I ask you how you can reconcile it with the personal integrity of the framers either of the Declaration of Independence or of the Federal Constitution, that they sanctioned a crime at the same time that they protested against it.

Mr. TRUMBULL. Mr. President, I am satisfied that I am not understood by the Senator from Alabama. I say that the negro has the same natural rights that I have; and now I say it is not a crime, under all circumstances, to hold a negro in slavery.

Mr. CLAY. Why, then, does the Senator's party denounce it as a twin relic of barbarism with polygamy? Is not that a crime? Do not your laws punish it? Do not the laws of my State punish it? And if Slavery is equal in iniquity with polygamy, why should not the laws of all the States punish it?

Mr. TRUMBULL. We would punish polygamy in Illinois as a crime; and we would punish the holding of a slave in Illinois as a crime.

Mr. CLAY. Will the Senator pardon me? I do not mean to be officious, and I do not intend to be offensive.

Mr. TRUMBULL. I do not take it so. I am very glad, indeed, to be interrogated. I wish to express my gratification at Senators' efforts to obtain explanations.

Mr. CLAY. I wish the Senator to explain whether, according to his code of ethics, or that of the party to which he belongs, it becomes any civilized, any Christian Government, to recognise crime; whether there be any circumstances under which crime can be justified, excused, or palliated?

Mr. TRUMBULL. Mr. President, I will not cavil about the word "crime." I do not call it a crime in citizens of the South to hold slaves at all.

Mr. CLAY. Is not polygamy a crime?

Mr. TRUMBULL. Polygamy is a crime under some circumstances, but not always a crime. I take it that polygamy is no crime in Turkey.

Mr. CLAY. Thank you for that concession, in this Christian country.

Mr. TRUMBULL. I think it is no crime in Turkey. It is a crime in our Christian country. We regard it so, but other nations do not regard it as a crime. I do not regard the holding of slaves as they are held in the Southern States of this Union, and in many other countries, as necessarily criminal. That is not the term I apply to it. I think it is a wrong to those persons who are so held, but it is a wrong which had better be endured than to do worse. It is better to be endured than to undertake to right it by committing a greater wrong and a greater evil.

Mr. CLAY. Then, if the Senator will pardon me, I understand him to maintain that right and wrong are merely conventional; that whether polygamy be a crime or not, depends merely upon the laws of society or upon the tone of moral sentiment of society.

Mr. TRUMBULL. Not entirely, Mr. President, do I concede them to be conventional. Many things, doubtless, are either criminal or innocent according to the circumstances; and when we speak of crime in human society or in political organizations, we mean some violation of the laws of the land; and I take it there are no laws of the land upon the subject of polygamy in some countries, and I suppose it would not, in that sense, be a crime in those countries. If the gentleman wants my opinion of it morally, which I presume he does not, of course I am very willing to express it.

Mr. CLAY. Will the Senator pardon me for interrupting him? Would not the taking of a human being's life without justifiable or excusable cause be a crime, independent of all statutory provision or legal enactment; and if so, by parity of reasoning, is not polygamy a crime? and if so, by the force of your own platform, which condemns Slavery equally with polygamy, is that not a crime, independent of all human legislation?

Mr. TRUMBULL. The taking of human life in the instance the Senator puts, unjustifiably, would undoubtedly be a great wrong and a crime, and so it would be a great wrong and a crime to deprive a person of his liberty without justifiable or excusable cause. It is always a natural wrong, but it is not, in my judgment, a crime in every instance. I have never so regarded it. This is my explanation of that part of the Declaration of Independence which declares that all men were created equal, and of the enunciation of the same principle in the platform of the Republican party. If it means anything else, I do not understand it, and the people of the State of Illinois do not understand it. It is the doctrine we have proclaimed there always, and the people of the State of Illinois who belong to the Republican party, belong to it as a party adopting the principles of the old Republican party; and as that old Republican party kept Slavery out of the Territories, believing it to be an evil, we desire to do the same thing, and for that purpose the present Republican party was organized, because of the change of the policy of the Government on the subject of Slavery, in undertaking to extend it.

I may omit to answer fully the Senator from Florida. I hope I shall not, and certainly I will not omit answering frankly, so far as I am able to do so, if I recollect the positions which he has assumed, for in this debate it is no interruption to me that gentlemen ask questions. I wish to deceive nobody. I have no prepared speech to make, and therefore it is no interruption to me. If I can afford information to any gentleman from the South, that shall disabuse his mind as to the objects and views of the Northern people, I shall consider that I am performing a service to my country in giving the information.

I have not been able to get through with what I designed to say in reply to the Senator from Florida, the Senator from Alabama having interposed some questions in the mean time, diverting my attention from him. I shall endeavor to answer him. The Republican party, as I understand, was organized with regard to the Territorial question; but if the Senator, when he says it is confined altogether to that, means to understand me as saying that the Republican party would not make itself efficient in preventing the violation of the law in the revival of the African slave trade, or anything of that kind, he misunderstands me. The Republican party, on this subject of Slavery, would prevent its extension, and it would enforce the laws equally in the North and in the South. While it would not interpose to prevent the owner of a slave from recapturing him in a free State, it would make itself active in preventing violations of the law in the Southern States by the introduction of negroes from the coast of Africa, and the revival of the African slave trade. We would administer this Government very differently from the manner in which it is now administered; and if we had control, the army and navy of the land would be as ready to arrest your vessels loaded with slaves, when they landed upon the Southern coast, as they are to arrest a negro that may be found loose somewhere in the city of Boston.

The Senator asked me the question distinctly, Was Slavery abolished by the Constitution of the United States? No, sir.

Mr. YULEE. No, sir; I did not ask that question. I asked the meaning of this clause in the Republican platform.

Mr. TRUMBULL. Perhaps I shall be able to answer; if not, when I get through, the Senator can repeat the question. He wanted to know if the slaves in Tennessee and Louisiana are freed by this platform. No, sir; the Senator certainly understands that.

Mr. YULEE. I do.

Mr. TRUMBULL. He wanted to know if the slaves are free in the District of Columbia by this platform. No, sir.

Mr. PUGH. May I ask the Senator whether he is speaking for himself or for the party?

Mr. TRUMBULL. I am speaking for myself; and as I understand——

Mr. PUGH. I thought you were interpreting the party.

Mr. TRUMBULL. I am giving my understanding of the Republican creed, and the way it is understood by the people of the Northwest, who are a conservative, Union-loving, Constitution-abiding people, loyal to the Constitution and to the Union, and are no ultraists in any sense of the word.

Mr. PUGH. Will the Senator permit me to ask him whether he considers Governor Chase, of Ohio, an exponent of the principles of the Republican party?

Mr. TRUMBULL. Mr. President, I consider that (the platform) the exponent of the principles of the Republican party, and not what any one man may say. It is the creed of one million three hundred thousand men, and Governor Chase may or may not precisely agree with me in his interpretation of every clause. I do not believe it possible there can be as much difference between us as there is between the Senator from Ohio with his popular-sovereignty dogma and the great Democratic party. [Laughter.]

Mr. PUGH. That is just what I want to find out; how much difference there is between the Senator and the rest of his party.

Mr. TRUMBULL. I do not believe there is so wide a difference as that.

Mr. YULEE. But the Senator wondered yesterday evening that I was unable to understand his platform.

Mr. TRUMBULL. It seems to me a plain platform. It has no Northern and Southern face, like your Cincinnati creed. We do not preach popular sovereignty in the North, and scout it as a humbug in the South.

Mr. PUGH. You do not preach it in the South at all.

Mr. TRUMBULL. No, sir; we do not preach it in the South at all; and yet the men who do not allow our principles to be proclaimed in the South, talk about sectionalism. A sectionalism so pure and unadulterated that it will not tolerate the exposition of the principles of its opponents at all where it is in power, talks to the other party about sectionalism!

I say that Slavery was not abolished in Tennessee and Louisiana by the Constitution. Why, sir, does not the Senator from Florida know that we acquired Tennessee by a deed of cession that prohibited the extension to it of that portion of the ordinance of 1787 which excluded Slavery? Slavery existed there, not by virtue of the Constitution creating it, but by virtue of local law, and that is the authority which establishes Slavery everywhere. Slavery can exist nowhere except by virtue of local law, and that is the reason why the person who owns a slave in a State cannot hold him as a slave, under the law of his State, in a Territory where Slavery has never been established. The Senator wants to know if Congress can confiscate his property. Surely not. That question cannot arise; he cannot hold the property there; he does not own the man; he voluntarily goes into a jurisdiction where there is no law to establish Slavery, and when he goes there the shackles of the slave fall off, not by virtue of the Constitution of the United States abolishing Slavery everywhere, but by the universal law of mankind, that this thing of Slavery is so odious that it can only be sustained by positive law.

Mr. YULEE. As I wish to understand the Senator perfectly as we proceed, I will ask him this question: When he spoke of the existence of Slavery in Tennessee by virtue of the local law, did he mean the local law of the Territory, or the local law as established and recognised by Congress by virtue of the compact with North Carolina?

Mr. TRUMBULL. I mean the local law existing in that Territory when it was ceded, and which Congress, in accepting, agreed not to interfere with.

The local law in Tennessee authorizing Slavery was not a law to which Congress gave existence; it was a law in existence before Congress had any jurisdiction over the Territory. The Constitution did not intervene by its terms to exclude Slavery, there being a local law in existence, not made by Congress, authorizing it. Congress had nothing to do with the making of that local law. It was there; men had a right to their slaves as property in the Territory before it belonged to the United States at all. Now, he wants to know whether Congress can confiscate that property. No—not if it is property; but if it was in a Territory where there had been no law establishing Slavery, and if, as he supposes, people from the Southern States exclusively go into such a Territory with their slaves, they do not hold them by virtue of any law when they get there, and it is no confiscation of property so to declare. They have no property in slaves in such a case.

Mr. YULEE. Suppose they make a law.

Mr. TRUMBULL. They cannot. That is the very thing the Republican party say they cannot do while in a Territorial condition. They have no right to do it. The creed of the Republican party, as I understand it, is, that you cannot extend Slavery, under the Federal Government, into the Territories of the United States. There may be Slavery in a country which does not belong to the United States; the United States may acquire that country, and may not abolish Slavery, because the right to hold slaves existed when the country was acquired; but it does not follow, that if the country was free when we acquired it, men could afterwards have property in slaves in it; and that is the distinction.

The Senator wants to know whether it is a part of the Republican creed to keep out of the Union a State tolerating Slavery, which applies for admission. Read the creed; is there any such word in it? Is there anything that looks like it? Why not ask me if it is a part of the Republican creed to keep out of the Union a State applying for admission into the Union, the Constitution of which provides that her people shall elect her own Governor? We have never said so. What right have you to assume any such thing? It is no part of our creed, as laid down in our platform, to refuse a State admission into this Union because she may or may not have Slavery. Look into it; see if you can find any such thing. Why, then, propound a question founded upon a hypothesis which has no foundation in the creed of the party?

If the Senator wants my individual opinion, he can have that. I have no concealments. I stated it here at the first session of Congress I served. I stated that it was not, with me, a fundamental principle that a State should not come into this Union as a slave State. I would regret the application of a State of that character; but I have adopted it as no part of my political faith, that under no possible circumstances shall a State be admitted into this Union that tolerates Slavery. The Republican party is not to be charged with having assumed the ground, that a State may not be admitted into the Union that has Slavery. The old Republican party, from which we learn our principles, did not keep slave States out, although they provided against the extension of Slavery into all territories, when they were not prohibited from so doing by the terms of cession; and if we do that, we will never, I trust, be troubled with the application of a slave State for admission.

The Senator says that the Supreme Court has decided that slaves may be legally held in a Territory. I deny it. The Supreme Court has decided no such thing. The Supreme Court has no power to lay down political doctrines in this country. It may decide a case that comes before it, and by the decision of the Court in that case I am willing to abide. The Court did decide that Dred Scott had no right to bring a suit in the United States courts, and that is all it decided. That decision is final as to him in that particular case; but, when the judges of the Court travelled out of the record, and undertook to lay down political principles for this Government, they departed, in my judgment, from the line of their duty, and the expression of their opinions is entitled to no more credit with me, upon political questions, than the expression of the opinion of the same number of gentlemen off the bench. Why, sir, there had been decisions involving the question of the right to govern the Territories before the present Chief Justice presided. Look back, sir, [Mr. MASON in the chair,] to the doctrine promulgated by your own Marshall, the ablest lawyer that ever sat on that bench, a Southern man. In one of his opinions, which is the opinion of the whole and not of a divided Court, he says, that in legislating for the Territories, Congress possesses the combined powers of the Federal and a State Government. If so, and if a State Government may prohibit Slavery, then Congress, possessing in a Territory the powers of a State Government and of the Federal Government combined, may do the same thing; and where is your reverence for the doctrines of the Supreme Court, when you attack that decision? Sir, for sixty years that was the doctrine of the country, acquiesced in by all parties. Why did you assail it, and open up this exciting question? I deny that any such decision has been made as that Slavery exists in a Territory, or that the owner of a slave has a right to take him to a Territory, and hold him there as a slave.

I believe, sir, that I have answered—I have certainly endeavored to do so—the questions which the Senator from Florida propounded to me.

Mr. YULEE. Is the Senator proposing to leave the subject?

Mr. TRUMBULL. Yes, sir; I propose to leave that point.

Mr. YULEE. I am very sorry to trouble the Senator. But suppose the inhabitants of a Territory chose to recognise Slavery, and to legislate with reference to the protection of that property; and, without undertaking to discuss with him whether the courts have already declared that the right of property in a slave is not changed by migration to a Territory, suppose a local law of the Territory authorizes it, and suppose the courts of the Territory and the courts of the United States sustain the legality of it, will then the party to which the gentleman belongs feel themselves bound to legislate for the destruction of the right asserted of property in slaves within that Territory? I am not speaking of territory in which there was any previous existence of Slavery, * * * but a Territory in which the inhabitants choose to recognise Slavery and to legislate for it, and in which the courts sustain it; would it be incumbent upon the gentleman's party under this platform to legislate to exclude it? That is what I want to know.

Mr. TRUMBULL. Mr. President, in my judgment, they should exclude it, as was done in the cases of Indiana and Illinois, when Territories, and whose inhabitants were refused permission to introduce Slavery when they asked it of Congress.

If the Supreme Court of the United States should make a decision so utterly variant from the repeated decisions of the courts in the Southern States, and of the former decisions of the Supreme Court itself, as to say that one person had a right to hold another as a slave in a Territory by virtue of any action of the inhabitants of a Territory, in defiance of Congress, I would acquiesce in the decision of the court as to the particular case. If A sued for his freedom, and the court decided that he was not entitled to it, I would not revolutionize the Government upon that; but it would be a decision in that case, and in that case only, and I would contest it on the morrow in the next. I would contest it day by day, until the court was reformed, and another Marshall put at its head, who should administer the law as our fathers made it.

Mr. YULEE. I do not ask the Senator's opinion. I ask him to expound the platform.

Mr. TRUMBULL. I have expounded it. It denies any such right. Your hypothetical case will never arise. We deny that a court will ever make such a decision; and if it should, we will resort to the constitutional means, to the ballot-box, to the people; we will appeal from the exposition of our political rights by men dressed in gowns to the great body of the people, who make Judges and Presidents too.

Mr. YULEE. You would legislate to exclude it?

Mr. TRUMBULL. We would legislate to exclude it; and the decision of a case would no more establish Slavery in a Territory, except as to the individual case, than has your decision as to Dred Scott, that he could not sue in the Federal courts, established the fact that Congress could not legislate to keep Slavery out of a Territory; a decision which scarcely a justice of the peace in the State of Illinois would have made. Why, sir, if an individual had come before one of our justices with a claim exceeding the jurisdiction of a justice of the peace, and the justice had examined it, and had seen that he had no jurisdiction, and then had gone on and investigated the case, and said how he would have decided if he had had jurisdiction, I think the whole community would have laughed at his folly. That is exactly what the Supreme Court of the United States has done in the Dred Scott case. The idea that the Supreme Court of the United States can establish political principles in this country is a new article in the creed of the Democratic party. It was not the former doctrine of the present Chief Magistrate of the country. It was not the doctrine of Thomas Jefferson. He regarded the Supreme Court as a set of sappers and miners, digging under the Constitution, who might in process of time subvert and destroy it.

Mr. YULEE. Now, then, I would turn the Senator's attention to another question. I asked whether, under the first clause of this platform, the Senator construed Slavery to be legally existing, or otherwise, in the District of Columbia, and in the forts and arsenals, and other places in which the exclusive jurisdiction of the United States prevailed by the Constitution. These are the words——

Mr. TRUMBULL. I will answer the question without troubling the Senator to read the platform. I conceive that in the District of Columbia the Constitution of the United States has not, *ex vi termini,* abolished Slavery, because it existed here, by virtue of local law, when the United States obtained jurisdiction over the District.

Now, sir, I think I have answered these gentlemen so that they cannot at any rate misapprehend my views, and I have done it without concealment or holding back at all; and, as I said, if I have been the means of disabusing the mind of a single Senator, or of a single person in the South who may ever take occasion to look over the desultory remarks I have made, I shall rejoice at it.

Having endeavored to show what the Republican platform is, having given my understanding of it, I wish to ask Southern Senators why is there such a persistence in choosing to misunderstand us? I do not charge that upon any particular Senator; but why is it that in the Southern States of this Union we are called Abolitionists. Would Senators induce their constituents to think more harshly of us than we ought to be thought of? What is to be gained by it? Is the South to gain anything by making its inhabitants believe, and inducing, if you please, the slaves to believe, that the great Republican party is ready to put knives and pistols into the hands of the slaves, to murder their masters? What will you have accomplished when you shall have induced such a belief among the white people of the South, or among the slaves of the South? Will you be more secure? Will there be any less likelihood of an insurrection, when you have circulated throughout the whole slave population the idea that the great mass of the people of the North are ready to arm them to slaughter their masters? Why not, then, I ask, treat us as brethren? Treat us fairly, take our platform as it is. When we say that all men are created equal, we do not mean that every man in organized society has the same rights. We do not tolerate that in Illinois. I know that there is a distinction between these two races, because the Almighty himself has marked it upon their very faces; and, in my judgment, man cannot, by legislation or otherwise, produce a perfect equality between these races, so that they will live happily together.

I have always been a Democrat; and yet, now I am denounced as a Black Republican, as an Abolitionist; for some of the Southern Governors, I believe, choose to call us all Abolitionists. I have changed no sentiment on the subject of Slavery since the time when I acted with the old Democratic party. I am no more averse to it now than I was then. I have lived amidst it, and would be as far as any Senator from interfering with this domestic relation where it exists in the States.

I inquired what gentlemen meant by talking about an inequality of rights between the North and the South; and about aggressions of the North upon the South; and when and where they were made. In reply, the Senator from South Carolina, instead of taking our platform as the exponent of our principles, adverted to what a single individual of the Republican party had said. Now, sir, does it comport with the candor and the fairness of that distinguished Senator, who is, I believe, ordinarily, a very candid and fair gentleman, to attribute to a great party in the country, which has declared its principles in Convention assembled, what any one individual member of the party may say are his own opinions?

The Republican party has declared no such principles as the Senator attributes to it. Would he mislead his people? Would he deceive himself?

Mr. CHESNUT. Mr. President——

The PRESIDING OFFICER, (Mr. MASON.) Does the Senator yield the floor?

Mr. TRUMBULL. Yes, sir.

Mr. CHESNUT. The Senator has been pleased to comment on a portion of the remarks which I made yesterday, as not presenting a candid view of the subject, as if I did not speak in candor.

Mr. TRUMBULL. I do not mean to impute a want of candor, in any offensive sense, to the Senator; but I think he has not fairly stated our principles.

Mr. CHESNUT. Mr. President, I merely rose to state, in response to what the Senator asked of me, whether I would take the opinion of a party from an individual, that ordinarily I would not; but when I find the party acting upon such principles generally; when I find him who is acknowledged as the distinguished leader of that party, and so admitted, I believe, everywhere, and I suppose among themselves, uttering his well-considered and elaborate opinions; opinions which have been promulgated, and which have had their effect upon the country; opinions which have never before been denied by the party; which have never before been questioned, so far as I am aware; which have never been responded to by the gentlemen who belong to that party, as not being the opinions of their party, I felt at liberty, and I think I was authorized in feeling myself at liberty, to hold them as the opinions, the well-considered opinions, of the leader of this great party in the North. That is the reason why I chose, upon the discursive debate of yesterday, having that speech before me, to predicate my remarks of the purposes and principles of that party upon the speech of that distinguished leader.

Mr. TRUMBULL. Mr. President, I wish to say that I acknowledge, and, so far as I know, the Republican party acknowledges, no man as its leader. However high my respect for the distinguished Senator from New York, not now with us, I do not acknowledge him as the leader of the Republican party; nor do I hold myself responsible for the opinions he may express. We acknowledge no leaders. Whether the views enunciated by the Senator from New York are correct or not correct, is not the question; if they differ from the creed of the Republican party as announced in its authoritative Convention, then they are not the creed of the party.

Mr. CHESNUT. May I ask the Senator one question?

Mr. TRUMBULL. Certainly.

Mr. CHESNUT. Does he repudiate those views of the Senator from New York?

Mr. TRUMBULL. I repudiate the construction that you have put upon those views. And now I wish to ask the Senator from South Carolina, who read from that speech, which I have here before me, if it comported exactly with his sense of fair dealing and propriety as a Senator of the United States, speaking in his place here for the information of the Senate and the country, and his own constituents in the South, to attribute to him such sentiments as these: "We (of the North) will subjugate you; give us the reins of power, and we will place you at our feet?"

Mr. CHESNUT. I quoted no such language as having been used by the Senator from New York. I quoted from the speech of the Senator from New York, in which he expressly stated, as the result of this "irrepressible conflict," that the wheat-fields and rye-fields of New York and Massachusetts would ultimately be tilled by slave labor, or that the sugar plantations of Louisiana and the rice-fields and cotton-fields of South Carolina must be tilled by free labor. That was the language of the Senator from New York.

Mr. TRUMBULL. I will ask the Senator, then, if it comports with his sense of fair dealing to a Senator from one of these United States, to quote that portion of the speech, and leave out this:

"On the other hand, while I do confidently believe and hope that my country will yet become a land of universal Freedom, I do not expect that it will be made so otherwise than through the action of the several States co-operating with the Federal Government, and all acting in strict conformity with their respective Constitutions."

Mr. CHESNUT. True, Mr. President, that part of the speech is there. * * * I quoted, from another speech, a portion which I thought bore strongly upon the recent occurrences; but from the speech from which the gentleman now quotes, I made a quotation expressly to show what was the purpose of the gentlemen, and what they had in view. I do not care by what means they seek to bring it about. They may take one means or another, but they have the end in view; and it is that which we resist, and which we will resist.

Mr. TRUMBULL. This is the speech where the term "irrepressible conflict" occurs; and if the Senator is satisfied to go before the country in the attitude of having quoted one portion of the speech, and given to it a meaning at variance with another portion which he has left out, wherein it is stated in express terms, by the Senator from New York, that he has no expectation that this country will all become free, except through the action of the States in a constitutional way, it is his privilege to do so. I draw his attention to it in fairness and in candor, as I have conducted this whole discussion on my part; and it seemed to me that it was, at least, due to the Senator who was not here, that his own explanation of the language which he had used should go along with what had been quoted; particularly as the Senator from South Carolina drew inferences which led him to use language wherein he spoke of subjugating the South, and placing them under the feet of the North, as if that were a legitimate deduction from the remarks which he quoted, though the Senator who made these remarks had himself taken occasion, in the same speech, to guard against such an interpretation.

Mr. CHESNUT. One word, by the permission of the Senator. I think, if the Senator will read that speech again, he will discover that, no matter what means may have been mentioned specifically, the speaker indicated to his audience, to the people of the North, that it is in their power; that this conflict is to be carried on; that through them and by their power they can produce this result. * * * I consider that I have done no injustice. I am willing to go before the country and before the world upon the question of fairness and justice to the views of the Senator from New York. * * *

Mr. TRUMBULL. I am sorry that the Senator from South Carolina, who usually speaks with so much candor, should not be willing that the qualifying remarks made by the Senator from New York should go out with those which he thought proper to quote, and especially when he put an interpretation upon them different from that of their author. But, sir, if he is satisfied that it shall go before country as he has stated it, that is a matter of taste and propriety with him.

One word in reply to the Senator from South Carolina, as to the constitutional question. He says, if Congress has sovereign power, and can exclude Slavery from a Territory, why may it not establish Slavery? I tried to answer that question some time ago. I shall not repeat the argument; but let me put a question in turn. The Congress can prohibit the establishment of a monarchy in a Territory; can it therefore establish a monarchy? It can prohibit murder; can it legalize murder? I suppose by a law of Congress we can and we do prevent murder in the Indian country; we may do so in a Territory. Can anybody pretend that, under the Constitution of the United States, Congress could sanction murder? Let me not be misunderstood, or my remark misapplied, by saying that I compare Slavery to murder. I have already said that Slavery may not be a crime at all. I put these as illustrations, to show that it does not necessarily follow that Congress can establish a thing because it can prohibit it. But I will not dwell on that.

Sir, the sentiments of the Senator from New York, which have been so much commented upon, are not new to this country. He is not the author of the declaration of this principle, that there is a conflict between right and wrong, between good and evil; nor is he the first person who has looked forward to the time when all the States should be free. Let me read to the Senate what the Father of his Country said upon this very subject. General Washington, in a letter written to General Lafayette, in 1798, said:

"I agree with you cordially in your views in regard to negro slavery. I have long considered it a most serious evil, both socially and politically, and I should rejoice in any feasible scheme to rid our States of such a burden.

"The Congress of 1787 adopted an ordinance which prohibits the existence of involuntary servitude in our Northwestern Territory forever. I consider it a wise measure. It met with the approval and assent of nearly every member of the States more immediately interested in slave labor. The prevailing opinion in Virginia is against the spread of Slavery into the new Territories, and I trust we shall have a Confederacy of free States."

What more than that is the declaration of the Senator from New York? Were these doctrines considered heretical in 1798? Did General Washington promulgate a principle which was to degrade the South, reduce it to subjection, trample its rights under foot? This principle then met the approbation of the people of the South; the prevailing sentiment of Virginia was against the spread of Slavery into new Territories, and such is the prevailing sentiment of the people of Illinois. Hear further, sir, what the founder of the old Republican party said upon this subject:

"With the morals of the people, their industry also is destroyed; for, in a warm climate, no man will labor for himself who can make another labor for him. This is so true, that, of the proprietors of slaves, a very small proportion indeed are ever seen to labor. And can the liberty of a nation be thought secure when we have removed their only firm basis—a conviction in the minds of the people that these liberties are the gift of God—that they are not to be violated but with His wrath? Indeed, I tremble for my country when I reflect that God is just; that His justice cannot sleep forever; that, considering numbers, nature, and natural means only, a revolution of the wheel of fortune, an exchange of situation, is among possible events; that it may become probable by supernatural influence! The Almighty has no attribute which can take side with us in such a contest."

That was the language of Thomas Jefferson, the great apostle of human liberty in this country. Again: Thomas Jefferson, in 1821, referring to a number of bills which had been introduced into the Legislature of Virginia, with regard to the emancipation of slaves, used this language:

"The bill on the subject of slaves was a mere digest of the existing laws respecting them, without any intimation of a plan for a future and general emancipation. It was thought better that this should be kept back, and attempted only by way of amendment whenever the bill should be brought on. The principles of the amendment, however, were agreed on; that is to say, the freedom of all born after a certain day, and deportation at a proper age. But it was found that the public mind would not yet bear the proposition, nor will it bear it even at this day. Yet the day is not distant when it must bear and adopt it, or worse will follow. Nothing is more certainly written in the book of fate, than that these people are to be free."

Where was the Senator from South Carolina in 1821, when Thomas Jefferson proclaimed that nothing was more certainly written in the book of fate, than that these people were to be free. Let me read further:

"Nor is it less certain that the two races, equally free, cannot live in the same Government. Nature, habit, opinion, have drawn indelible lines of distinction between them. It is still in our power to direct the process of emancipation and deportation peaceably, and in such slow degree as that the evil will wear off insensibly, and their place be, *pari passu*, filled up by free white laborers. If, on the contrary, it is left to force itself on, human nature must shudder at the prospect held up. We should in vain look for an example in the Spanish deportation or deletion of the Moors. This precedent would fall far short of our case.

"I consider four of these bills, passed or reported, as forming a system by which every fibre would be eradicated of ancient or future aristocracy, and a foundation laid for a Government truly republican."

Where, then, was the feeling which is now exhibited, that the South ought to dissolve the Union on account of the utterance of such sentiments, and especially when the Senator from New York has taken the pains to guard against the inference that he was for using any other than constitutional and legal means in co-operation with the States in getting rid eventually, in the far distant future, of this thing of Slavery. It will be seen that the idea is not new nor peculiar to the Senator from New York. It had its origin in Virginia years ago; and I trust that an idea foreshadowed by Mr. Jefferson will hereafter become, although it is not now, part of the creed of the Republican party—I mean the idea of the deportation of the free negro population from this country. I trust the Republican party will make it part of its creed, that this Government should procure some region of country, not far distant, to which our free negro population may be taken. I fear the consequences, which Jefferson so eloquently prophesied, unless that is done. The negro population is increasing at a rapid rate. I agree with the sentiment of Mr. Jefferson, that two races which are marked by distinctive features cannot live peaceably together without one domineering over the other, especially when they differ in color. The free negro population of this country is a great evil now. I believe it to be the interest of the black population that they should go to some country where they may develop their powers, and where there shall be no superior race to domineer over them, and that it is the duty of this Government to use its means for the purpose of freeing our country of that portion of this population that is willing to go. I think, in that way, this thing of Slavery may eventually be got rid of. Thousands of masters would be willing to free their slaves, if there was any provision for them when freed; but in most of the States where Slavery exists, laws have been passed prohibiting emancipation except on condition that the emancipated slave shall leave the jurisdiction of the State. Where are they to go? The North does not want a free negro population; the South will not have them. The consequence is, that emancipation has nearly ceased. If, however, a country contiguous were provided, where the free negro population of the United States who were willing might go—and I think they would soon all be willing to leave, if they could go under the fostering care of this Government until they became sufficiently numerous to protect themselves and establish a Government of their own—we might establish a system which, in process of time, not in your day, sir, nor in mine, nor perhaps in the day of the coming generation, but in future time, would relieve us of the black population, and prevent consequences which we shudder to contemplate. I cannot so well express my views on this point as by quoting from a speech made by a distinguished Senator from Kentucky, now no more, before the American Colonization Society. He said:

"We are reproached with doing mischief by the agitation of this question. The Society goes into no household to disturb its domestic tranquillity; it addresses itself to no slaves, to weaken their obligations of obedience; it seeks to affect no man's property. It neither has the power nor the will to affect the property of any one contrary to his consent. The execution of its scheme would augment, instead of diminishing, the value of the property left behind. The Society, composed of freemen, concerns itself only with the free. Collateral consequences we are not responsible for. It is not this Society which has produced the great moral revolution which the age exhibits. What would they, who thus reproach us, have done?"

Now, see how his language fits the declarations of the Senator from South Carolina, who finds such fault with the idea of ultimate emancipation:

"If they would repress all tendencies towards liberty and ultimate emancipation, they must do more than put down the benevolent efforts of this Society. They must go back to the era of our liberty and independence, and muzzle the cannon which thunders its annual joyous return. They must revive the slave trade, with all its train of atrocities."

Ay, sir, revive the slave trade as we now see it being revived!

"They must suppress the workings of British philanthropy, seeking to ameliorate the condition of the unfortunate West Indian slaves. They must arrest the career of South American deliverance from thraldom. They must blow out the moral lights around us, and extinguish that greatest torch of all, which America presents to a benighted world, pointing the way to their rights, their liberties, and their happiness. And when they have achieved all these purposes, their work will be yet incomplete. They must penetrate the human soul, and eradicate the light of reason and the love of liberty. Then, and not till then, when universal darkness and despair prevail, can you perpetuate Slavery, and repress all sympathies and all humane and benevolent efforts among freemen in behalf of the unhappy portion of our race who are doomed to bondage."

That, sir, was the language of Henry Clay in regard to the colonization of the free blacks in Africa. It seems to be impracticable to transport this great population to Africa. Let us obtain a country nearer home; and to show the sympathy of the North for the South, I think I may say—I know I may say for the people whom I represent—we will contribute liberally of our means to relieve the country of the free negro population, and of all slaves who may be voluntarily emancipated, by planting them in some contiguous country by themselves. I hope that may become the policy of the Republican party. I hope that we shall join hands with the South; that, instead of reproaching each other, instead of saying anything which would create a misunderstanding between different sections of the Union, we may come together as our fathers did of old in their struggle for independence, and, side by side as brothers, adopt a policy which, if it shall not eventually deliver the country from the only element which ever seriously threatened its peace, shall at least prevent its spread and increase, and at the same time furnish the means of relieving the country of the evils of a large free negro population. By such a course we may lay the foundation for continued and permanent prosperity.

WASHINGTON, D. C.
BUELL & BLANCHARD, PRINTERS.
1859.

www.ingramcontent.com/pod-product-compliance
Lightning Source LLC
LaVergne TN
LVHW020642110826
845149LV00004B/1316

* 9 7 8 1 4 1 8 1 9 0 0 8 8 *